COOKING WEEDS

For Mum

COOKING WEEDS

A VEGETARIAN COOKERY BOOK

Vivien Weise

PROSPECT BOOKS

2004

First published in Great Britain in 2004 by Prospect Books, Allaleigh House, Blackawton, Totnes, Devon TQ9 7DL.

An edition of this book, entitled *The Gourmet Weed Cookery Book*, was first published in Germany by VIWO Verlag in collaboration with Martin Feindt in 2002.

British Library Cataloguing in Publication Data:
A catalogue entry for this book is available from the British Library.

ISBN 1-903018-30-7

Cover designed by Andras Kaldor.

Typeset by Tom Jaine.

Printed and bound in Great Britain at the Cromwell Press, Trowbridge, Wiltshire.

Acknowledgements

I would like to thank all those people who have helped me with this book: Jennie Marx for her work correcting and proofreading; Sabine Babbel-Monzel for her translations and advice; Uwe Turek for help with graphics, design and computers; and last but not least my wonderful husband Wolf for his photographs, his counsel and the support he has given all my projects.

Sevenig/Our
August, 2004

Comfrey – the stalk of the young plant is a substitute for asparagus.

TABLE OF CONTENTS

Characteristics of the recipes in this book

QUICKLY PREPARED
Almost all the recipes can be prepared in a short time. There are only a few ones which take longer than half an hour to cook.

INEXPENSIVE
The recipes work out really cheaply because the ingredients growing in the garden, field and forest are free.

SIMPLE
Most of the recipes are easy to prepare and not too much of a challenge for beginners.

HEALTHY
Cooking with weeds is extremely healthy because they contain large amounts of vitamins and minerals (see tables).

Preface

M any people do not realise when they walk across their lawn or through fields and forests that there is healthy food in abundance, all around them. The food is weeds – or wild vegetables as they could be described. Flowers and buds can also be eaten and are not only tasty but can be used to decorate the plate.

For many years now I have been giving weed cookery courses. We identify and pick the plants and then, working with my recipes, turn them into gourmet dishes. I use well over 100 weeds in my dishes. My continued success with the courses is proof of how tasty and versatile weeds are.

Weeds also grow in abundance in every front and back garden, however small. They turn up on balconies and in pots, much to some people's annoyance. Whilst weeding (whether in the field, garden or on the balcony) the edible weeds can go in a basket for the kitchen and the inedible ones (of which there are not many) can go in a bucket for the compost heap – thus killing two birds with one stone by harvesting one's meal and weeding simultaneously!

All weeds are of course organic and full of goodness, containing many more vitamins and minerals and much more protein than cultivated vegetables (see tables). As an example, compare stinging nettles to lettuce: there are 333 mg of vitamin C in 100 g of stinging nettles as opposed to 13 mg of vitamin C in 100 g of lettuce. This positive comparison holds good for all weeds and their vitamins, minerals and protein. Another great advantage with weeds is that they are practically never eaten by insects or bugs and never get choked by other plants. They are extremely nutritious, no work at all, organic and there in abundance waiting to be picked. What more could one ask for!

It is important, however, that the source of weeds is an area untreated by weed-killer and not contaminated by animal excrement. Cooking with weeds as well as cultivated vegetables gives one a far greater variety of dishes. In the Middle Ages many weeds were cultivated especially for use, like the carrot, cauliflower etc. are today.

In this book I have used a variety of weeds: well-known ones for beginners (e.g. daisies, stinging nettles, dandelions etc.) and less well-known ones (e.g. smooth sow thistle and nipplewort) for those who want to venture a bit further and try out some new and exciting tastes. The weeds should be harvested before or during flowering but never after they have flowered. One really should stick to this rule. There is one exception in this book, the lesser celandine which should only be harvested before flowering as it becomes inedible whilst and of course after flowering.

My aim in writing this book is to help the reader to reduce his or her food bill and at the same time cook healthy, nutritious food. Added to this, I would like to awaken people's interest in weeds which have been looked down upon in every respect for a long time. Unfortunately our great-grandmothers' knowledge has been all but lost by the following generations.

I would also like people to realise what fun it is to create rather different recipes from those normally cooked. I have kept most of the recipes in this book quick and simple as housewives and cooks of today do not want to slave over a hot stove for hours in order to produce a meal. I have also used some well-known old favourites, for example lasagne or pizza, to show that weeds are well-suited to such recipes, too. There are also some exotic recipes, brought back from our many trips to all corners of the globe.

Apart from practice in weed-recognition, the only extra skill required of the reader is knowledge of where to buy other ingredients. Most are readily available in high-street stores. All others will be found in health-food shops.

Bistort
Polygonum bistorta

Bistort Zucchini Stew

Serves 4 as a main course

1 onion
5 large cloves of garlic
60 g butter
320 g pearled barley
200 g tomatoes
500 ml vegetable stock
50 g bistort
400 g courgettes
soy sauce
lemon juice
pepper, salt, paprika
some single cream

Chop the onion, press the garlic and fry them in half the butter until translucent. Add the barley and brown it, stirring all the time. Slice the tomatoes and mix them into the barley/onion mixture. Add the vegetable stock. Bring to the boil, then turn down the heat and let simmer for 20 minutes. After 10 minutes add the finely chopped bistort. Slice the courgettes thinly and fry them in another pan with the rest of the butter on a moderate heat until they are light brown. Season with soy sauce to taste. When the barley is cooked, season with lemon juice, pepper, salt and paprika. Finally, stir in some single cream and add the courgettes to the stew. Reheat before serving.

Bistort – a very pretty plant with pink flowers and a delicious taste into the bargain.

Bistort Bolognese

Serves 2 as a main course

Very popular with children.

 120 g green spelt grains
1 litre of vegetable stock
2 large onions
butter
4 carrots (about 250 g)
200 g leeks
3 handfuls bistort
3 tomatoes
2–3 leaves fresh lovage
3 cloves garlic
nutmeg, pepper
3 tablespoons tomato purée

Stir the green spelt into the vegetable stock, bring to the boil and let simmer gently for 20 minutes. In the meantime chop the onions finely and fry them in butter until translucent.

Grate the carrots, slice the leeks and add both to the onions. Then chop the bistort coarsely, cut the tomatoes into cubes and add to the vegetable mixture. Chop the lovage very finely, crush the garlic and stir them into the vegetable sauce. Season with nutmeg and pepper to taste.

Drain the green spelt and mix it into the vegetables. Then stir in the tomato purée. Let the sauce simmer for another 10 to 15 minutes until it is thick enough. If it is too thick, add some water. Serve with whole-wheat spaghetti and a little grated cheese.

Comfrey
Symphytum officinale

Weeds for salad

The following weeds make excellent salad vegetables in any combination and at different times of the year: red clover, white clover, dead nettle, chickweed, <u>sorrel</u>, nipplewort, smooth sow thistle, fat hen, garden arrach, common mallow, daisy, <u>wild garlic</u>, ground elder, ribwort plantain, silver weed, <u>lady's smock</u>, hogweed, rosebay willowherb, <u>mugwort</u>, <u>sweet cicely</u>, bistort, the lesser celandine, yarrow, comfrey buds, ox-eye daisy, goosegrass, dandelion, <u>ground ivy</u>.

Any hard stalks or old leaves should not be used. This also applies to cooked weeds. The weeds underlined are spicy or have a strong taste and should be used sparingly.

Comfrey Salad

Serves 4 as a salad

Use only the young shoots of comfrey for the salad because they become hard and leathery the older they get.

3 handfuls comfrey (young shoots)
1 good handful cuckoo flower or lady's smock (Cardamine pratensis)
1 onion
2 apples
juice of one lemon
1 clove garlic
1 glass of red wine
pepper
sour cream
1 tablespoon olive oil

Chop the comfrey and the cuckoo flower finely. Cut the onion into small cubes. Chop the apples into small chunks and trickle the lemon juice over them.

For the dressing crush the garlic into the red wine and add some pepper. Gently stir in sour cream with a fork until there are no lumps left. Finally add the oil. Pour the dressing over the salad and mix well.

Comfrey Zucchini with Sorrel Sauce

Serves 4 as a main course

Sunflower seeds can be used instead of the pine nuts. The potatoes must still be hot when squeezed through the potato ricer.

Vegetables
500 g potatoes
4 courgettes (about 750 g)
salt
butter for frying and greasing
75 g grated Emmental cheese
75 g comfrey
2 egg yolks
60 g pine nuts
50 g freshly grated Parmesan cheese
nutmeg, pepper, paprika
Sauce
2 handfuls sorrel
1 onion
150 ml single cream
butter for frying
50 g butter
lemon juice

Peel and boil the potatoes. Cut each courgette lengthwise in halves and hollow them out. Chop the removed courgette flesh and boil it together with the potatoes for 5 minutes, then drain the mixture. Salt the courgette halves and fry them briefly in butter on both sides. Arrange the courgettes in a greased ovenproof dish and sprinkle them with the Emmental cheese.

Squeeze the hot potatoes together with the courgette flesh through a potato ricer. Chop the comfrey very finely. Add it to the potato mixture, together with the egg yolks, half the amount of pine nuts and the Parmesan cheese. Mix everything well and season with nutmeg, pepper and paprika. Spoon or pipe the mixture into the courgette halves. Bake in the oven at 175°C (350°F, gas mark 4) for 15 minutes. Then sprinkle the remaining pine nuts on top.

For the sauce, chop the sorrel finely. Cut the onion into small cubes and fry in butter until translucent. Add the sorrel and the single cream and let them simmer for 5 minutes with the lid off. Add 50 g butter and mix in the blender. Taste and season with lemon juice.

This is the best way to chop weeds finely.

Comfrey Hamburgers

Serves 3 or 4 as a main course

The healthy alternative to conventional hamburgers!

6–8 thick square slices of wholemeal bread, or pitta bread
100 g green spelt grains
1 large cup vegetable stock
4 handfuls comfrey leaves (with flowers, if you like)
1 handful mugwort
4 tiny leaves ground ivy
1 onion
butter for frying
1 teaspoon thyme, dried
1 teaspoon oregano, dried
1 teaspoon mixed herbs
1 teaspoon tomato purée
3 cloves garlic, crushed
1 egg
1 teaspoon French mustard
salt, pepper
For the bread
butter, mustard, tomato ketchup, mayonnaise, slices of tomato
and onion

Toast the bread. Cut into each slice from one side so that a pocket suitable for stuffing is created. This is easier with pitta bread.

Grind the green spelt coarsely and dry-fry it until it is a very pale brown. Add the vegetable stock and bring to the boil. Then turn down to a low heat and leave to simmer for 15 minutes.

Put some of the comfrey leaves aside and chop the others finely, as well as the mugwort and the ground ivy. Cut the onion into small cubes. Fry the onion in butter, then add the chopped weeds and the dried herbs. Stir in the tomato purée and add some water to avoid burning (be careful that you do not use too much water, otherwise the mixture cannot be shaped into burgers). Simmer for 10 minutes. Shortly before the weeds are done add the crushed garlic.

Mix the weeds well with the green spelt and the egg. Taste and season with mustard, salt and pepper. Add some flour if there is too much fluid in the mixture. Form into round flat burgers and fry them in vegetable oil on both sides until they are golden brown.

Now take the comfrey leaves put aside beforehand and fry them separately, 2 for each burger. Put one on either side of each burger. Season the bread to taste, like a conventional hamburger, with butter, mustard, tomato ketchup, mayonnaise, etc., and fill it with the burger and the comfrey leaves, adding tomato and onion slices if you like.

Comfrey African Style

Serves 4 as a main course

1 large onion
1 tomato
2 good handfuls comfrey (stalks, leaves, flowers)
butter for frying
$^1/_2$ teaspoon chilli powder
400 ml coconut milk (tinned)
salt

Cut the onion and the tomato into small cubes. Take the leaves and flowers off the comfrey stalks. Peel the stalks. Chop everything finely. Fry the onion in butter and season with the chilli powder. Add the tomato cubes and cook for a few minutes. Then stir in the comfrey and cook until done.

Finally add the coconut milk and warm it up. Taste and season with salt. Serve with rice.

Comfrey Hazelnut Paste

The hazelnut butter used in this recipe is available in health-food shops.

1 large onion
200 g comfrey leaves
50 g butter
3 small tomatoes
1 teaspoon wild marjoram or oregano
salt, pepper
a pinch of chilli powder
some water
2 cloves of garlic
1 tablespoon whole-wheat flour
4 teaspoons hazelnut butter

Cut the onion into rings and chop the comfrey leaves coarsely. Melt the butter in a frying pan and fry the onion rings until they are translucent. Slice the tomatoes and add them to the onions. Season with wild marjoram, salt, pepper and chilli powder. After two minutes stir in the comfrey and simmer the vegetable mixture with the lid on. From time to time add water to the vegetables so that they do not burn. Shortly before the comfrey leaves are cooked (after 7–15 minutes) add the garlic (cut into very thin slivers). Sprinkle on the flour and blend it well into the mixture. Let it cool slightly. Then pour the vegetables into the blender and liquidize them together with the hazelnut butter. If you want a very smooth paste, press it through a fine sieve in order to remove the fibres. If the paste is too thin, just pour it back into the frying pan. Heat it up, stirring all the time, to evaporate some of the liquid and thicken the paste.

Serve on freshly baked bread.

Minerals

Content of water (%) and of minerals (in mg/100 g of edible part).
K = Potassium; P = Phosphorus; Mg = Magnesium; Ca = Calcium; Fe = Iron.

Vegetables	Water (%)	K (mg)	P (mg)	Mg (mg)	Ca (mg)	Fe (mg)
Chinese cabbage	95.4	202	-	11	40	0.6
Lettuce	95.0	224	33	11	37	1.1
Chicory	94.4	192	26	13	26	0.7
Lamb's lettuce	93.4	421	49	13	35	2.0
Swiss chard	92.2	376	39	-	103	2.2
White cabbage	92.1	227	28	23	46	0.5
Red cabbage	91.8	266	30	18	35	0.5
Cauliflower	91.6	328	54	17	20	0.6
Spinach	91.6	633	55	58	126	4.1
Curly kale	86.3	490	87	31	212	1.9
Brussels sprouts	85.0	411	83	22	31	1.1
Average	91.7	342.7	48.4	21.7	64.6	1.4
Weeds						
Chickweed	91.5	680	54	39	80	8.4
Dandelion	89.9	590	68	23	50	1.2
Daisy	87.5	600	88	33	190	2.7
Fat hen	86.9	920	80	93	310	3.0
Coltsfoot	84.8	670	51	58	320	3.8
Stinging nettle	84.8	410	105	71	630	7.8
Bistort	84.0	580	74	69	100	3.9
Good King Henry	81.7	730	95	66	110	3.5
Hogweed	79.8	540	125	75	320	3.2
Rosebay willow herb	75.0	450	94	81	150	2.7
Average	84.6	617.0	83.4	60.8	226.0	4.0
Daily requirement for an adult (in mg)		3-4,000	800	300-350	800	13-18

Reference: Auswertungs- und Informationsdienst für Ernährung, Landwirtschaft und Forsten e. V. (AID): Wildgemüse. *Broschüre Nr. 1182 des AID-Verbraucherdienstes, Bonn, 1987, S. 8.*

Common Mallow
Malva sylvestris

Common Mallow 'Corned Beef'

Serves 4 as a main course

3 handfuls common mallow (leaves and flowers)
200 g carrots
200 g potatoes
2 medium onions
200 g cabbage
$^1/_2$ cup celery leaves, finely chopped
500ml strong vegetable stock
1 tablespoon yeast flakes
100 g ground hazelnuts
1 cup red wine

Chop the common mallow finely, dice carrots and potatoes, and chop the onions and cabbage coarsely. Cook the vegetables together with the celery in the vegetable stock for about 20 minutes and drain them. Add yeast flakes and hazelnuts and stir well.

Place the mixture in an ovenproof dish, baste it with the wine and bake it in the oven at 200°C (400°F, gas mark 6) for 10 minutes until it becomes light brown.

Common Mallow Sauce with Cucumber

700 g cucumber
butter
1 onion
4 cloves garlic
olive oil
50 g common mallow leaves
100 ml vegetable stock
500 ml single cream
10 g grated ginger
lemon juice
nutmeg
pepper, salt

Cut the cucumber into cubes. Fry the cucumber cubes in some butter until they are tender. Remove with a slotted spoon and reserve the liquid. Rinse the cucumber cubes with very cold water in order that they do not continue to cook and become too soft.

Chop the onion very finely and slice the garlic thinly. Fry both in olive oil until the onion is translucent. Cut the common mallow leaves in fine strips and stir them into the pan. Add the vegetable stock and the reserved liquid. Bring the sauce to the boil and add half of the single cream. Bring back to the boil and let simmer until the sauce is thickening. Stir from time to time and season with grated ginger, lemon juice and nutmeg. Gradually add the remaining cream. Continue to simmer until sauce has thickened. Season to taste.

Warm the cucumber cubes in the sauce before serving with rice.

Daisy
Bellis perennis

Daisy Dandelion Salad

Serves 4 as a salad

Not only the flowers but also the tiny leaves of daisies are delicious.

4 handfuls daisies (leaves and flowers)
2 handfuls dandelion (leaves, stalks and flowers)
2 spring onions
3 tablespoons lemon juice
nutmeg, pepper, salt
4–5 tablespoons sunflower oil
30 g sunflower seeds

Wash the daisies and chop the washed dandelion finely. Chop the onions very finely and stir them into the lemon juice. Season with nutmeg, pepper and salt. Finally whisk the oil into the dressing.

Gently roast the sunflower seeds in a small amount of sunflower oil. Blend them into the salad just before serving.

Daisy Salad with Mushrooms

Serves 4 as a salad

300 g mushrooms
3 handfuls daisies (leaves and flowers)
nutmeg
1 tablespoon white vinegar, pepper, salt
3 tablespoons olive oil

Slice the mushrooms finely. Mix with the washed daisies. For the dressing, grind some nutmeg into the vinegar and stir in pepper, salt and the oil. Pour the dressing over the salad and mix thoroughly.

Daisy Soup

Serves 4

Put some of the nicest daisy flowers aside and use them for garnishing the soup.

1 litre water
herb salt
4 handfuls daisies
60 g semolina
60 g butter
1 large onion, finely chopped
a few lovage leaves, finely chopped
pepper
lemon juice
4 tablespoons crème fraîche

Bring the water to the boil, add the salt and the daisies. Let simmer for 4 minutes. Drain through a sieve, reserving the water. Finely chop the cooked daisies.

Dry-fry the semolina in a pan. Melt the butter in a saucepan and fry the finely-chopped onion. Gradually add the semolina and the daisies. Heat the mixture for some time, stirring well. Gradually add the reserved daisy-water. Taste and season with finely chopped lovage, pepper and lemon juice.

Blend in the crème fraîche before serving.

Daisy Ginger Soup

Serves 4

4 handfuls daisies (leaves and flowers)
1 litre vegetable stock
2 onions
butter for frying
40 g green ginger

Put aside a few flowers for garnishing. Boil the other daisies for 3 minutes in the vegetable stock. Drain them through a sieve, reserving the stock.

Chop the onions coarsely and fry them in butter until translucent. Add the vegetable stock. Chop the ginger, add it to the stock and boil up again for a short time. Let cool slightly, then liquidize the soup.

Chop the cooked daisies and add them to the soup. Serve in soup plates garnished with the flowers.

Vitamin A

Content of vitamin A (carotin) in micro-grams/100 g of edible part.

Vegetables		Weeds	
Red cabbage	5	Daisy	160
Cauliflower	6	Sorrel	215
Cabbage	7	Coltsfoot	250
White cabbage	7	Hogweed	360
Chinese cabbage	13	Chickweed	383
Leeks	58	Lesser celandine	390
Brussels sprouts	67	Rosebay willow herb	490
Lettuce	130	Dead nettle	539
Chicory	215	Common mallow	606
Broccoli	370	Ground elder	684
Cress	360	Stinging nettle	740
Swiss chard	590	Great burnet	830
Lamb's lettuce	650	Good King Henry	948
Curly kale	680	Red clover	1156
Spinach	700		
Carrot	2000		

Average	**257**	**Average**	**554**
(without carrot)			

Reference: Auswertungs- und Informationsdienst für Ernährung, Landwirtschaft und Forsten e. V. (AID): Wildgemüse. Broschüre Nr. 1182 des AID-Verbraucherdienstes, Bonn, 1987, S. 10.

Dandelion
Taraxacum officinale

Dandelion Salad with Banana Yoghurt Sauce

Serves 4

3 good handfuls dandelion (leaves, stalks and flowers)
1 onion
2 medium bananas
300 g yoghurt

Chop the dandelion finely. Chop the onion very finely and mash the bananas. Make a dressing of the yoghurt, banana and onion. Finally, mix the dressing with the dandelion.

Dandelion Salad with Blood Oranges

Serves 4

150 g dandelion (leaves, stalks and flowers)
4 blood oranges
1 onion
3 tablespoons lemon juice
1–2 teaspoons honey
pepper, nutmeg
3 tablespoons sunflower oil
30 g flaked almonds

Chop the dandelion coarsely, divide the oranges into segments and cut the onion into thin rings. For the dressing mix the lemon juice with honey and season with pepper and nutmeg. Stir in the oil. Pour the dressing over the salad.

Dry-fry the almonds until they are golden brown. Sprinkle them over the salad. Do not serve immediately but allow to marinate in a cool place for half an hour.

Dandelion Flowers in Batter

Serves 4 as a first course

This starter has to be prepared during the day and when the sun is shining, otherwise the dandelion flowers are closed.

75 g flour
100 ml milk
salt
1 teaspoon baking powder
30 dandelion flowers
oil for deep-frying

Blend flour, milk, salt and baking powder to form a soft batter. Flatten the flowers slightly with your hands. Dip the flowers into the batter and deep-fry.

Dandelion stalks as a spring tonic

Dandelions, especially the stalks, contain bitter-tasting substances which are good for the liver. Because of this it is a good idea to eat a few stalks every day in spring.

Dandelion Rice Salad

Serves 3 as a main course

250 g rice (2 cups)
4 cups vegetable stock
1 small onion
3 handfuls dandelion (flowers, leaves, stalks)
2 tablespoons desiccated coconut
8 tablespoons oil
6 tablespoons single cream
3 teaspoons fresh coriander, chopped
juice of 1 lemon
$^{1}/_{2}$ cup vegetable stock
herb salt and pepper
1 small tin sweet corn, drained
100 g grated hard cheese

Boil the rice in the vegetable stock. In the meantime chop the onion and the dandelion very finely. Make a dressing of the rest of the ingredients, except the rice, dandelions, sweet corn and cheese. When the rice is cold, blend it with the sweet corn and mix well with the dressing. Finally fold in the cheese.

Allow to marinate for half an hour before serving.

Dandelion Noodle Salad

Serves 4 as a main course

600 g whole-wheat noodles
2 good handfuls dandelion (flowers, leaves, stalks)
1 onion
8 tablespoons oil
2 tablespoons balsamic vinegar
2 teaspoons Worcester sauce
salt, pepper
6 tablespoons pumpkin seeds
desiccated coconut
dandelion flowers for garnishing

Boil, then drain the noodles and allow to cool down. Put some of the dandelion flowers aside for garnishing (this decoration is of course edible as well). Chop the remaining dandelion and the onion very finely.

For the dressing, mix oil, vinegar, onion and Worcester sauce and season with pepper and salt. Mix the noodles with dandelion and pumpkin seeds, then add the dressing and mix well. Sprinkle desiccated coconut over the salad and garnish with the flowers.

Allow to marinate for half an hour.

Dandelion – all parts of the plant can be eaten.

Dandelion Potato Salad

Serves 4 as a main course

600 g potatoes
2 good handfuls dandelion (flowers, leaves, stalks)
1 handful sorrel
1 medium onion
3 tablespoons yoghurt
2 tablespoons oil
2 tablespoons vinegar
4 tablespoons mayonnaise
salt, pepper
1 cup vegetable stock

Scrub the potatoes and leave the skins on. Boil the potatoes and slice them when cooled down. Chop the dandelion, sorrel and onion finely and mix with the potatoes.

Make a dressing of yoghurt mixed with oil, vinegar and mayonnaise. Season with salt and pepper.

Pour the vegetable stock over the potatoes, add the dressing and mix well. Allow to marinate for half an hour before serving.

Dead nettle – the flowers taste sweet.

Dead Nettle Lasagne

Serves 4 as a main course

Filling
2 onions
butter for frying
3 carrots (about 200 g)
200 g celeriac
1 teaspoon each of basil and oregano
2 tomatoes
2 tablespoons tomato purée
3 big handfuls dead nettles
2 cloves garlic
250 ml vegetable stock
Roux
50 g butter, 50 g flour
625 ml milk
1 teaspoon vegetable stock powder
pepper, nutmeg
Lasagne
250 g lasagne
200 g matured Gouda cheese, grated

Fry the onions in some butter until translucent. Grate the carrots and the celeriac coarsely and add them to the onions, together with basil and oregano. Continue to fry on a low heat. Slice the tomatoes and after about 5 minutes add them to the other vegetables. Stir in tomato purée, dead nettles and the crushed garlic. Add the vegetable stock. Cook for 10 to 15 minutes.

To make the roux, melt the butter in a saucepan, on medium heat, and let it froth up for a moment. Stir in the flour with a whisk and heat up. Add the milk and bring to the boil, stirring continuously. Season with vegetable stock powder, pepper and nutmeg.

Depending on the type of lasagne, it may be necessary to cook the noodles before use. Follow the instructions given on the packaging. Grease an ovenproof dish with butter and cover the bottom with lasagne. Spoon a layer of filling on top, then grated cheese and the roux. Repeat the procedure ending up with a topping of grated cheese. Bake in the centre of the oven at 180°C, 350°F, gas mark 4, for about 25 minutes.

Dead Nettle
Lamium album

Dead Nettle Curry

Serves 2 as a main course

2 medium onions
2 cloves garlic
butter for frying
100 g desiccated coconut
1 piece of fresh ginger (about the size of a large garlic clove)
3 teaspoons fresh coriander, chopped
3 teaspoons cumin powder
$^1/_2$ teaspoon chilli powder
2 medium carrots
2 medium tomatoes
3 big handfuls dead nettles
2 tablespoons tomato purée
250 ml water
some single cream

Cut the onions and the garlic into very small cubes and fry them in some butter on a medium heat. Add the coconut. Grate the ginger finely. Stir in the ginger and all the spices and continue to fry. Keep stirring to prevent burning. Slice the carrots, dice the tomatoes and chop the dead nettles finely. Mix carrots, dead nettles, tomatoes and tomato purée into the pan. Add the water and simmer until cooked. Finally stir in a dash of cream.

Serve with rice or chapattis.

Dead Nettles in Cheese Sauce

Serves 4 as a main course

This dish is delicious with brown rice.

1 large onion
50 g butter
1 large clove garlic
3 handfuls dead nettles
250 ml vegetable stock
3 tablespoons wholemeal flour, finely ground
1 teaspoon paprika
1 teaspoon herb salt
pepper
100 g grated hard cheese
125 g crème fraîche
lemon juice

Chop the onion finely and fry it in butter. Stir in the crushed garlic and the chopped dead nettles. Continue to fry for a short time. Add the vegetable stock and cook for about 15 minutes. Sprinkle in the flour and stir well. Bring to the boil again. Add more vegetable stock if the mixture is too thick. Add the paprika, the seasoning and the cheese. Finally stir in the crème fraîche. Some lemon juice may be added to taste.

Dead Nettle Savoury Cake

Serves 4 as a main course

This is not a sweet cake but a savoury main dish.

 3 handfuls dead nettles
1 large onion
3 cloves garlic
2 carrots
1 cup grated kohlrabi
1 cup grated hard cheese
1 tablespoon vegetable stock powder
2 eggs
1 cup hazelnuts, pounded or chopped
1 cup breadcrumbs

 Chop the dead nettles finely, cut the onion into small cubes and crush the garlic. Grate the carrots finely, like the kohlrabi and the cheese. Dissolve the vegetable stock powder in very little water. Mix all the ingredients thoroughly together. Press the mixture into a greased ovenproof dish and bake at 180°C, 350°F, gas mark 4, for 45 minutes.

Chopping weeds finely

Especially for those not used to eating weeds, it is important to chop them very finely because the leaves are often harder and thicker than, for example, lettuce leaves.

Dead Nettle Aubergine Spread

700 g aubergines
1 large onion
2 carrots (about 100 g)
1 large tomato
3–4 handfuls dead nettles
2 handfuls ground ivy
oil for frying
1 tablespoon wild marjoram
2 tablespoons single cream
herb salt

Cut the aubergines lengthwise into halves. Roast them on a baking tray on the bottom shelf of the oven at 180°C for about 15 minutes until they are cooked. Scoop out the centre of the aubergines. Reserve the flesh and the skin separately. Chop the onion finely, grate the carrots, cut the tomato into cubes and chop up the weeds finely. Heat some oil and fry the onion and the carrots on a low heat for about 5 minutes. Stir in the tomato, the weeds and the marjoram. Add a tablespoon of single cream to make the spread softer and cook until tender. Mix in the aubergine flesh and season with herb salt. Add some more cream if necessary but take care that the paste does not become too thin. Spoon the spread into the aubergine skin and serve with freshly baked bread.

Elder
Sambucus nigra

Elderberry Purée

Serves 2 as a dessert

400 g elderberries
50 g sultanas
3 tablespoons honey
1 cup stewed apple
2 tablespoons hazelnuts, pounded or chopped
2 tablespoons rum
150 g yoghurt

Wash the elderberries and remove the stalks. Boil the berries in some water until tender. Put half a cup of elderberries aside for garnishing. Strain the remaining berries through a sieve to form a purée. Reheat the berry purée, adding sultanas, honey and stewed apple. Let simmer gently for 2 to 3 minutes. Remove from heat and leave to cool. Stir the hazelnuts, the rum and the yoghurt into the cream and garnish with the reserved elderberries.

Elderberry Jelly with Meringues

Serves 4–6 as a dessert

Jelly

400 g elderberries
1 cup stewed pears
250 ml red wine
4 tablespoons honey
1 tablespoon cornflour
1 cup whipping cream

Meringues

4 egg whites (cooled in the fridge)
3 tablespoons liquid honey

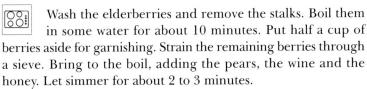

Wash the elderberries and remove the stalks. Boil them in some water for about 10 minutes. Put half a cup of berries aside for garnishing. Strain the remaining berries through a sieve. Bring to the boil, adding the pears, the wine and the honey. Let simmer for about 2 to 3 minutes.

Blend the cornflour with some water. Remove berry mixture from the heat and stir in the cornflour. Reheat, stirring all the time until the mixture is thick. Add more cornflour, if necessary. Leave to cool.

To make the meringues, whisk the egg whites until very stiff, trickling in the honey little by little. Whisk for at least 10 minutes. Long whisking and the low temperature of the egg whites will make the meringues look nicer. Cover the tray with greaseproof paper and place the meringues on it, using a tablespoon. Bake them in the oven at 100°C, 210°F, gas mark 1, for about 1 to 1 $^{1}/_{2}$ hours until firm.

Whip the cream and fold it into the jelly. Serve it together with the meringues.

Elderflower Pancakes

Makes 12 small pancakes

3 eggs, separated
200 g flour
300–400 ml milk
vegetable oil
12 small or medium elderflower heads
cinnamon, sugar

Mix egg yolks, flour and milk together to make a firm batter. Leave to stand for a moment. Whisk the egg whites until stiff and fold them into the batter. Heat the oil in a pan. Put one portion of the batter into the oil and dip one of the flower heads in. Fry on a medium heat until golden brown, then cut off the stalks with kitchen scissors. Toss the pancake and fry on the other side until golden brown and firm. Bake the other pancakes in the same way. Serve sprinkled with cinnamon and sugar.

Elderflower.

Elderflower Cake

Serves 4 as a dessert

5 handfuls elderflowers
200 g butter
200 g honey
3 eggs, separated
100 g almonds
400 g flour
15 g baking powder
³/₄ teaspoon cinnamon
50 ml milk

Remove and discard elderflower stalks and put the flowers aside. Whisk the butter until creamy. Add the honey and stir well. Separate the eggs and add the egg yolks to the butter. Keep stirring to make a smooth consistency. Chop the almonds finely. Mix the flour with the baking powder, the almonds and the cinnamon. Add the milk and the butter cream and mix together. Carefully stir the elderflowers into the mixture. Whisk the egg whites until stiff and fold them into the mixture. Place the mixture into a greased baking tin. Bake in the centre of the oven at 180°C, 350°F, gas mark 4, for 30 minutes.

Protein

Content of protein - in g/100 g of edible part

Vegetables		Weeds	
White cabbage	0.2	Chickweed	1.5
Chicory	0.4	Daisy	2.6
Red cabbage	0.4	Sorrel	2.8
Cabbage	0.6	Dandelion	3.3
Lettuce	0.9	Dead nettle	4.1
Spring leeks	1.0	Fat hen	4.3
Chinese cabbage	1.3	Good King Henry	5.3
Lamb's lettuce	1.8	Stinging nettle	5.9
Autumn spinach	2.1	Ground elder	6.7
Spinach	2.5	Common mallow	7.2
Brussels sprouts	2.8		
Curly kale	3.0		
Average	**1.4**	**Average**	**4.4**

Reference: Auswertungs- und Informationsdienst für Ernährung, Landwirtschaft und Forsten e. V. (AID): Wildgemüse. *Broschüre Nr. 1182 des AID-Verbraucherdienstes, Bonn, 1987, S. 11.*

Fat Hen
Chenopodium album

Fat Hen Gazpacho

Serves 4 as a first course

A delicious starter for a hot day.

1 good handful fat hen
1 red pepper (about 200 g)
$^1/_2$ cucumber (about 200 g)
2 tomatoes (about 200 g)
1 small onion
1 $^1/_2$ cups tomato purée
$^1/_2$ cup tomato juice
1–2 tablespoons olive oil to taste
1–2 cloves garlic to taste
herb salt, pepper
lemon juice

Chop the fat hen very finely. Chop the red pepper, cucumber, tomatoes and onion coarsely. Liquidize them in the blender, little by little adding tomato purée, tomato juice and olive oil. Crush the garlic. Mix all ingredients together. Season with herb salt, pepper and lemon juice and serve chilled.

Fat Hen Cream Sauce with Potatoes

Enough for 2 servings

The amount of potatoes depends on one's own taste.

unpeeled potatoes
1 onion
1 clove garlic
butter for frying
2 handfuls fat hen
125 ml vegetable stock
500 ml single cream
lemon juice
pepper
a pinch of ginger powder
1 teaspoon vegetable stock powder

Boil the potatoes for about 20 minutes. In the meantime chop the onion and the garlic finely and fry in butter. Chop the fat hen and fry it together with the onion briefly. Add the vegetable stock and cook for about 10 minutes until tender. Stir in the single cream little by little. Continue to stir until the mixture has thickened. Taste and season with the lemon juice, pepper, ginger powder and vegetable stock powder. Serve with the hot potatoes.

Goosegrass
Galium aparine

Goosegrass Salad

Serves 4 as a salad

Only use goosegrass when it is very young, otherwise the stalks are tough and stringy.

3 handfuls goosegrass
2 handfuls mixed weeds, e.g. ground elder, red and white
   clover, ribwort plantain, chickweed
1 handful herbs for seasoning, e.g. lemon balm, ground ivy,
   peppermint, parsley, basil
4 radishes
1 onion
juice of 1 lemon
200 ml tomato juice
nutmeg
paprika
pepper, salt
olive oil

Cut the goosegrass and the other weeds into thin strips. Chop the herbs very finely. They will be part of the dressing. Slice the radishes thinly and chop the onion in very small cubes. Mix the lemon juice into the tomato juice. Add the spices, the seasoning and the chopped herbs, stirring all well together. Finally add the oil, stirring all the time. Mix the weeds, the radishes and the onion and pour the dressing over the salad.

Goosegrass Soup

Only use goosegrass when it is very young, otherwise the stalks are tough and stringy.

3 handfuls goosegrass
2 handfuls mixed weeds, e.g. ground elder, ribwort plantain,
    dead nettle, dandelion, comfrey, yarrow, clover, daisies
weeds for seasoning, e.g. ground ivy, wild garlic, lady's smock
herbs for seasoning, e.g. lovage, thyme, marjoram, lemon balm,
    peppermint, dill, parsley, chives
1 onion
1–2 cloves garlic
oil for frying
1–2 tablespoons wholewheat flour, finely ground
approx 750 ml vegetable stock
pepper
crème fraîche

Wash the weeds and herbs and chop them coarsely. Chop the onion and the garlic and fry it in oil until golden. Add the herbs and weeds. Sprinkle in some flour, the amount depending on the required thickness of the finished soup. Add the vegetable stock and cook for about 15 minutes. Let cool slightly, then liquidize until the soup is smooth. Add pepper to taste. Serve with a spoonful of crème fraîche.

Ground Elder
Aegopodium podagraria

Ground elder – a highly nutritious vegetable.

For most people ground elder in one's garden is one of the most hated weeds of all because it is impossible to get rid of. So do not fight it, eat it! And be happy that it is there for the taking.

Ground Elder Layered Pancakes

Serves 3 as a main course

Pancakes
500 ml milk
salt
100 g flour
4 eggs
50 g rolled oats
60 g butter
peanut oil for frying
Filling
750 g spinach
2 handfuls ground elder
$^1/_2$ handful ground ivy
a few wild garlic leaves
20 g butter
100 g sour cream
300 g mozzarella

For the pancakes, make a batter of milk, salt and flour and leave to stand for at least 20 minutes. Separate the eggs. Blend the yolks and whisk the whites until stiff. Roast the rolled oats in butter and leave to cool. Blend them and the egg yolks into the batter, then fold the egg whites in. Heat the oil and fry the pancakes (about 3 to 4 minutes on either side). Place the pancakes on a paper towel in order to drain off the fat.

For the filling, chop spinach and ground elder coarsely, and ivy and wild garlic finely. Fry in butter for five minutes. Stir in the sour cream and simmer for 5 minutes.

Stack the pancakes in an ovenproof dish, with a layer of filling between each pancake. Crumble the mozzarella and sprinkle on top. Bake in the oven at 200°C, 400°F, gas mark 6, for 6 to 8 minutes.

Ground Elder with Creamy Sorrel Sauce

Serves 4 as a main course

Vegetables
700 g pumpkin
2 onions
2 cloves garlic
50 g ground elder
2 tablespoons olive oil
125 ml vegetable stock
pepper
Sauce
1 handful sorrel
150 g sour cream
paprika
pepper, herb salt

Peel the pumpkin, remove the seeds and cut the flesh into bite-sized cubes. Chop the onions and the garlic very finely. Wash the ground elder, discarding the stalks and yellow leaves. Chop coarsely. Fry the garlic and three quarters of the chopped onions in oil until golden. Stir in the pumpkin cubes and the ground elder and add the vegetable stock. Cover and cook on moderate heat for 10 minutes until the pumpkin is tender but not too soft. Season with a good amount of pepper.

For the sauce, cut the sorrel into very thin strips. Blend it into the sour cream, together with the remaining onions. Season with paprika, pepper and herb salt.

Divide the cooked vegetables into four portions and pour the sour cream sauce over each portion.

Ground Elder with Cheese Soufflé

Serves 4 as a main course

Vegetables
750 g ground elder
500 g comfrey
500 g tomatoes
1 large onion
60 g butter
some water
1 tablespoon flour
2-3 tablespoons lemon juice
pepper, salt

Soufflé
100 g Emmental cheese
60 g Parmesan cheese
4 eggs
60 g butter
nutmeg
butter for greasing 4 thick china teacups

Wash the weeds, discard the tough stalks and dry the leaves with a kitchen towel. Carve a cross into the skin of each tomato, blanch them in boiling water for a few seconds and rinse with cold water. Now it is easy to peel them. Cut them in halves and discard the seeds, then chop the flesh into cubes. Chop the onion finely and the weeds coarsely. Heat the butter in a saucepan, letting it foam up. Add the onion and the leaves, cover and cook for about 8 minutes. Add some water from time to time so that it does not burn. Add the tomatoes and continue to cook for a short time. Mix the flour with water until you have a paste, then thicken the mixture with it. Add the lemon juice and season with salt and pepper.

For the soufflé, grate the cheese finely. Separate the eggs and whisk the butter until creamy. Stir the egg yolks in one at a time, then fold in the cheese. Add some nutmeg to the egg whites and whisk them until stiff. Fold them into the mixture. Grease the teacups with butter and spoon the soufflé mixture into the cups, about three-quarters full. Bake in the preheated oven at 175°C, 350°F, gas mark 4, for about 20 minutes. Turn out on 4 plates and serve with the vegetables.

Ground Elder Potato Spread

300 g potatoes
4 tablespoons olive oil
50 g red peppers
$^1/_2$ small onion
2 good handfuls ground elder
a few wild marjoram leaves (or dried marjoram)
6 black olives, stoned
1 large tomato
herb salt, pepper

Boil and mash the potatoes and blend the oil into the warm purée. Chop the peppers and the onion finely. Chop up ground elder and wild marjoram and cut olives and tomato into small cubes. Mix all ingredients together. Taste and season with pepper and salt. Serve on thinly sliced toast.

Hogweed with bud – a wonderful substitute for broccoli.

Hogweed in Rolled Chapatti

1 serving

The Indian chapatti is a thin, flat round loaf, dry fried (i.e. without any fat or oil). The amount of water needed will vary depending on the type of flour you use. Just add the amount necessary to make the dough soft and smooth.

Makes 1 chapatti roll

100 g flour
salt
water

1 small onion
butter
2 handfuls hogweed
1 handful dead nettles
1 handful stinging nettles
1 small carrot
½ handful dandelion, heads and leaves
2 slices avocado
1 tablespoon mayonnaise
1 teaspoon Dijon mustard
2 tablespoons bean sprouts and sunflower seeds, mixed
1 large lettuce leaf
a pinch of salt (optional)

For the chapatti, mix the flour and the salt. Add water, stirring all the time, until you get a soft dough. Leave to stand for half an hour. Roll out the dough, forming it into a round, thin loaf. Heat a frying-pan without any fat on the hotplate until it is very hot. Put the loaf into the pan for about 30 seconds, but do not allow to burn. Then take a dry cloth, screwed up into a ball, and press it hard on every part of the chapatti's surface. Turn the chapatti over and repeat the procedure. When

65

the dough is pressed it should form bubbles. If not, the pan is not hot enough or the chapatti has not been in the pan long enough. In that case turn it over once more.

For the filling, chop the onion finely and fry it in butter. Cut the hogweed, dead nettles and stinging nettles coarsely, add them to the onion and let everything cook together. In the meantime grate the carrot, chop up the dandelion and slice the avocado.

Cover the chapatti with mayonnaise and mustard to your own taste. Then spread the boiled weeds, the carrot, dandelion, avocado, bean sprouts and sunflower seeds evenly on the chapatti and cover it with the lettuce. Sprinkle with salt according to taste.

Carefully roll the chapatti up and serve.

Hogweed
Heracleum sphondylium

Hogweed with Chilli Cheese Sauce

Serves 4 as a main course

5 handfuls hogweed
250 ml vegetable stock
2 onions
oil for frying
2 cloves garlic
¹/₂ teaspoon chilli powder
pepper
1 cup breadcrumbs
2 cups milk
100 g Gouda cheese
a dash of single cream
juice of 1 lemon

Chop the hogweed into small pieces and boil it in about half the vegetable stock. In the meantime prepare the sauce. Chop the onions finely and fry them in the oil. Crush the garlic and add it to the onions. Mix in chilli, pepper and then the breadcrumbs. Add the milk and bring the sauce to the boil. Stir in the rest of the vegetable stock and let simmer for 10 minutes.

Sprinkle the cheese into the mixture. Add more milk if the sauce is too thick. Stir in the cream and boil up again. Finally, add the lemon juice and pour the sauce over the hogweed before serving.

Hogweed Pancakes

Serves 4 as a main course

150 g flour
a good 250 ml milk
2 eggs
salt
oil for frying
250 g Swiss chard
1 medium onion
5 handfuls hogweed
1 large tomato
2 cloves garlic
butter for frying
1 tablespoon paprika
1 cup water, salted
3 heaped tablespoons Parmesan cheese

Make a batter of flour, milk, eggs and salt, fry 4 pancakes in oil and keep warm in a cool oven. Chop the Swiss chard and the onion finely, cut the hogweed coarsely. Cut the tomato into cubes. Fry onion and crushed garlic in butter and stir in the paprika. Add Swiss chard and hogweed and fry gently for a couple of minutes. Then mix in the tomato cubes, add the water and cook for 15 to 20 minutes. Finally, stir in the cheese. Spread the vegetable mixture on each pancake and roll it up. Return it to the oven and serve hot.

Hogweed Nut Loaf

Serves 4 as a main course

1 large onion
5 handfuls hogweed
butter
400 g carrots
100 g kohlrabi
200 g courgettes
100 g Emmental cheese
1 large tomato
75 g walnuts
¹/₂ cup breadcrumbs, butter
1 tablespoon vegetable stock powder
2 tablespoons oil

Chop the onion and the hogweed finely and fry in butter. Grate the carrots, kohlrabi, courgettes, and the cheese. Slice the tomato. Chop the walnuts very finely. Fry the breadcrumbs in butter until they are golden brown. Mix all the ingredients together including the vegetable stock and the oil and put the mixture into a well-greased, ovenproof dish. Bake in the oven at 250°C, 480°F, gas mark 10, for about 40 minutes.

Hogweed Pulao

Serves 4 as a main course

Pulao is an Indian rice dish.

1 large onion
butter
3 teaspoons coriander
3 teaspoons cumin powder
2 teaspoons curry powder
1 teaspoon ground ginger
¹/₂ teaspoon ground cinnamon
¹/₂ teaspoon ground cloves
1 pinch chilli powder
300 g rice
2 tablespoons tomato purée
750 ml vegetable stock
2 carrots
3 handfuls hogweed

Cut the onion into small cubes. Fry it gently in butter on a low heat, together with the spices. When the onion is translucent add the rice and the tomato purée. Heat it up on a high heat for a moment, stirring all the time. Do not allow to burn. When the rice is slightly browned, add the vegetable stock. Let it simmer gently until the rice is half cooked (about 10 minutes). In the meantime cut the carrots into cubes, then add the hogweed and the carrots and let them all cook together.

Lesser Celandine
Ranunculus ficaria

Lesser Celandine Salad with Carrot Cream

Serves 4 as a salad

The lesser celandine should only be used before it is in flower as during and after flowering it becomes slightly poisonous.

250 g carrots
100 ml single cream
pepper, salt
nutmeg
juice of half a lemon
2 handfuls lesser celandine

Grate the carrots very finely. Mix pepper, salt, nutmeg and lemon juice with the cream. Mix the lesser celandine with the carrots, then the dressing with the vegetable mixture.

A life-saver

The lesser celandine is of utmost importance because it is one of our first spring flowers and is very effective in treating scurvy. It was used to treat sailors in the Middle Ages when they returned home from a long sea voyage suffering from vitamin C deficiency.

The lesser celandine should only be used before it flowers as during and after that the plant is slightly poisonous and inedible.

Lesser Celandine Mushroom Salad

Serves 4 as a salad

The lesser celandine should only be used before it is in flower as during and after flowering it becomes slightly poisonous.

150 g mushrooms
2 handfuls lesser celandine
1 clove garlic
juice of 1 lemon
2 sprigs tarragon
2 sprigs basil
pepper
walnut oil
mild vinegar

Wipe the mushrooms and wash the lesser celandine. Slice the mushrooms thinly with a sharp knife. Crush the garlic into the lemon juice. Grind the tarragon and basil in a pestle and mortar. Add to the garlic and lemon, together with some pepper. Stir in enough walnut oil to carry the dressing and add a dash of vinegar. Pour the dressing over the salad and mix well.

Lesser Celandine Cream Soup

Serves 4

The lesser celandine should only be used before it is in flower as during and after flowering it becomes slightly poisonous.

1 onion
butter for frying
3 handfuls lesser celandine
2 handfuls yarrow
2 handfuls ground elder
2 handfuls sorrel
2 raspberry leaves
2 strawberry leaves
ground ivy
3 boiled potatoes
butter for frying
750 ml vegetable stock
some single cream

Chop the onion and fry it in butter until translucent. Chop the weeds and the berry leaves coarsely and dice the potatoes. Fry together with the onion for a short time. Add the vegetable stock, bring to the boil and simmer for 10 minutes. Liquidize the soup and add a dash of cream.

Lesser Celandine Potato Salad

Serves 4 as a main course

The lesser celandine should only be used before it is in flower as during and after flowering it becomes slightly poisonous.

 1 kg potatoes
1 large onion
2 handfuls lesser celandine
3 tablespoons vinegar
fresh parsley
mixed herbs
salt, pepper
paprika
nutmeg
4–5 tablespoons olive oil

Scrub and boil the potatoes. In the meantime chop the onion and the lesser celandine finely. Make a dressing of the remaining ingredients. Slice or dice the potatoes, with or without skin. Mix them with onion and the lesser celandine. Pour the dressing over the salad and mix well. Allow to marinate for at least half an hour.

Nipplewort
Lapsana communis

Nipplewort Green Spelt Soup

Serves 2 as a main course or 4 as a first course

5 handfuls nipplewort
1 handful prickly sow thistle
1 small handful wild marjoram
1 handful silverweed
¼ handful mugwort leaves
1 large onion
1 red pepper
butter
1 litre vegetable stock
125 g green spelt
250 ml water
salt, pepper

Chop nipplewort, sow thistle, wild marjoram, silverweed, mugwort, onion and pepper finely. Fry them all in butter, add the vegetable stock and cook until tender.

In the meantime grind the green spelt finely into flour. Stir it into the weeds, add the water and bring to the boil, stirring well. Let cool slightly, then liquidize the soup and simmer for 3 to 4 minutes. Taste and season with salt and pepper.

Nipplewort Minestrone

Serves 4 as a first course

4 handfuls nipplewort
1 small carrot
2 tomatoes
1 large onion
3 cloves garlic
1 litre vegetable stock
50 g wholemeal noodles
salt, pepper, nutmeg
a pinch of cayenne pepper
$^1/_2$ handful ground elder for garnishing

Chop the nipplewort very finely. Cut the carrot and tomatoes into small cubes. Chop the onion finely, crush the garlic and fry them in oil until translucent. Stir in carrots, tomatoes and nipplewort and add the vegetable stock. Bring to the boil. Add the noodles and salt, pepper, nutmeg and cayenne and let simmer for about 10 minutes. Serve the soup sprinkled with the finely chopped ground elder.

Nipplewort Crème Fraîche

1 good handful nipplewort and smooth sow thistle
125 g crème fraîche
salt, pepper

Remove tough stalks from the weeds and use only young, delicate leaves. Chop the nipplewort and the smooth sow thistle very finely and mix them with the crème fraîche. Taste and season with pepper and salt. Serve on bread.

Nipplewort African Style

Serves 2 as a main course

2 onions
1 tablespoon vegetable oil
1 tablespoon peanut butter
2 tomatoes
5 handfuls nipplewort
¹/₂ teaspoon chilli powder
¹/₄ litre vegetable stock

Chop the onions finely. Mix the oil and the peanut butter well together in a pan. Heat carefully (on a medium heat), add the onions and fry gently. Cut the tomatoes into cubes and chop the nipplewort finely. Add the tomatoes to the peanut butter mixture and stir in the chilli powder. Finally, add the nipplewort and the vegetable stock. Cook for 5 to 10 minutes and serve with rice.

Nipplewort Hungarian Stew

Serves 4

2 onions
500 g potatoes
2 cloves garlic
1 litre water
3 tablespoons tomato purée
2 teaspoons marjoram
2 teaspoons paprika
salt, pepper
5 handfuls nipplewort
1 tablespoon wholewheat flour
2 cups sour cream

Cut the onions into small, the potatoes into bigger cubes. Crush the garlic. Put into a large saucepan, add the water and cook for 10 minutes. Stir in tomato purée, marjoram, paprika and seasoning. Add the finely chopped nipplewort. Cook for another 10 minutes. Stir in the flour and bring to the boil for a short time. Remove from the heat and mix the sour cream into the stew.

When to pick

One can pick any edible weed before flowering, and most of them during flowering. (There are exceptions, e.g. the lesser celandine must only be used before flowering.)

Ox-eye Daisy
Leucanthemum vulgare

Ox-eye Daisy Salad

Serves 4

2 handfuls ox-eye daisies (flowers and leaves)
2 handfuls mixed weeds, e.g. greater plantain, ribwort
plantain, chickweed, milk thistle, daisies, fat hen, ground elder
1 handful weeds for seasoning, e.g. ground ivy, lady's smock,
garlic mustard, wild garlic, lemon balm
1 onion
1 orange
1 clove garlic (optional)
juice of ½ lemon
salt, pepper
3 tablespoons olive oil

To prepare the weeds and daisies, cut off any tough stalks and discoloured leaves. Remove the thistle thorns with scissors. Cut the weeds into thin strips and chop the weeds for seasoning finely. Mix together.

For the dressing, chop the onion finely. Peel and chop the orange. Crush the garlic into the lemon juice and dissolve the salt in it. Add some pepper and stir in the onion and orange, then finish with the olive oil. Pour the dressing over the salad and mix well. Allow to marinate for at least 20 minutes.

Ox-eye Daisy Pizza

Serves 4–6 as a main course

Dough

250 g flour
20 g fresh yeast
1 teaspoon honey
125 ml milk
salt
1 tablespoon olive oil

Filling

70 g ox-eye daisies
70 g fat hen
1 handful wild marjoram
5 tomatoes
1 onion
some butter
200 g crème fraîche
250 g grated Emmental cheese
75 g grated Parmesan cheese
2 cloves garlic, crushed
pepper, salt

It is important that all ingredients for the dough are slightly warm. Put the flour into a bowl and make a well in the centre. Dissolve the honey in the warm milk and pour into the well. Crumble the yeast into the well and dissolve in the liquid. Leave to rise in a warm but not hot place for 10 to 20 minutes. Knead the yeast mixture, flour, salt and olive oil together to make a smooth dough. Leave to rise for another 10 to 15 minutes.

For the filling, take about 10 ox-eye daisy flowers and put them aside for garnishing. Mince the remaining ox-eye daisies together with the fat hen and the wild marjoram. Carve a cross into the skin of each tomato, blanch them in boiling water for a few seconds and rinse with cold water. Now it is easy to peel them. Chop them coarsely. Chop the onion finely and fry it in butter. Add the weeds and the tomatoes and cook with lid off until the paste is thick Stir in the crème fraîche. Continue to cook if the sauce is still too thin. Melt the cheese in the mixture, which will also thicken the sauce. Season with crushed garlic, pepper and salt.

Knead the dough again and roll it out on a greased baking tray. Spread the sauce evenly over the dough. Arrange the reserved flowers on top. Bake the pizza in the middle of the oven at 200°C (400°F, gas mark 6) for about 30 minutes.

Ox-eye Daisy Spread

1 large carrot (about 150 g)
1 small beetroot
1 onion
50 g butter
1 handful ox-eye daisies
1 handful mugwort
1 teaspoon ginger powder
pepper, salt
2 large cloves garlic
1 tablespoon whole-wheat flour
juice of 1 lemon

Grate the carrot and beetroot or cut them into matchsticks. Cut the onion into rings. Melt the butter in a pan and fry the onion for a short time. Add carrot and beetroot and fry for about 7 minutes with lid on. Take care not to burn, adding some water if necessary. Add the chopped weeds and cook for another 5 minutes.

Season with ginger powder, pepper, salt and thinly sliced garlic. Sprinkle the flour over the mixture and stir it in. Simmer for another 5 minutes. Add the lemon juice. Let cool slightly, and then blend it. If you want a very smooth paste you can also press it through a fine sieve in order to remove the fibres. If the paste is too thin put it back into the pan and reheat, stirring all the time, until it is has thickened. Serve on toast.

Ox-eye daisy salad looks pretty decorated with the flowers.

Ox-eye Daisy Sauce

Sufficient for 4 servings

Very good with potatoes or rice.

 400 ml water
1 handful ox-eye daisy leaves
50 g butter
1 onion
1 clove garlic
butter for frying
30 g fine oatmeal
salt and pepper
2 teaspoons grated ginger
2 teaspoons lemon juice
2 tablespoons white wine

Bring the water to the boil in a saucepan. Blanch the ox-eye daisy leaves in the boiling water for 5 minutes, strain and chop them finely. Put the water aside, it will be needed in the next step. Chop the onion and the garlic finely and fry them in butter until translucent. Remove the saucepan from the heat and stir in the oatmeal. Reheat, stirring all the time, then add the reserved hot water. Continue to stir, adding salt, pepper and ginger and bring to the boil. When the sauce is thick and smooth, season with lemon juice and white wine.

Ribwort Plantain
Plantago lanceolata

Ribwort Plantain Potato Pizza

Serves 4–6, in one baking tray

1 kg potatoes
1 egg
1 tablespoon flour
olive oil & tomato purée to coat the pizza base
1 large onion
2 cloves garlic
4 handfuls ribwort plantain
2 handfuls fat hen
1 handful ground elder
1 teaspoon oregano, dried
1 teaspoon basil, dried
1 teaspoon marjoram, dried
1 teaspoon chives, dried
2 tablespoons tomato purée
salt, pepper
2 large tomatoes
80 g grated Parmesan cheese
200 g grated Gouda cheese

Cook the potatoes and mash them. Mix in the egg and the flour. Grease the baking tray with olive oil and spread the purée evenly, 1 to 2 cm high. Bake in the oven just below the centre at 225°C (430°F, gas mark 7) for 20 minutes. Then spread oil and tomato purée on it. Chop the onion finely and crush the garlic. Chop ribwort plantain, fat hen and ground elder finely. Quickly brown the onion, garlic and dried herbs, then add the weeds and cook for 2 to 3 minutes. Take care not to overcook. Add 2 tablespoons tomato purée and season with salt and pepper.

Spread the mixture evenly on the potato pizza. Slice the tomatoes and place them on top. Trickle olive oil over it and sprinkle with cheese. Bake in the oven at 225°C (430°F, gas mark 7) for 20 minutes.

Ribwort Plantain Omelette

Serves 1

1 small onion
2 eggs
salt, pepper
1 handful ribwort plantain
oil for frying

Chop the onion finely and fry it in a pan. Whisk the eggs, adding salt and pepper. Chop the ribwort plantain finely and stir it in. Pour the mixture into the pan. Fry the omelette until the first side is golden brown and firm. Then toss it and cook the other side.

Chopping knife – a demi-lune is ideally suited to chopping weeds finely.

Vitamin C

Content of vitamin C in micro-grams/100 g of edible part.

Vegetables		Weeds	
Asparagus	21	Dandelion	115
Peas	25	Sorrel	117
Leeks	30	Lesser celandine	131
Lamb's lettuce	35	Garden arrach	157
Chinese cabbage	36	Chervil	179
Swiss chard	39	Good King Henry	184
Cabbage	45	Ground elder	201
White cabbage	46	Fat hen	236
Red cabbage	50	Hogweed	291
Spinach	52	Stinging nettle	333
Cauliflower	70	Rosebay willow herb	351
Curly kale	105	Great burnet	360
Broccoli	114	Silverweed	402
Brussels sprouts	114		
Average	**49**	**Average**	**210**

Reference: Auswertungs- und Informationsdienst für Ernährung, Landwirtschaft und Forsten e. V. (AID): Wildgemüse. *Broschüre Nr. 1182 des AID-Verbraucherdienstes, Bonn, 1987, S. 9.*

Ribwort Plantain Aubergine Dish

Serves 3 as a main course

1 handful ribwort plantain
400 g aubergines
1 large tomato
100 g kohlrabi
200 g carrots
1 medium onion
oil
2 teaspoons basil, dried
2 teaspoons dill, dried
2 teaspoons chives, dried
300 ml vegetable stock
3 teaspoons tomato purée
1 cup single cream
salt

Chop the ribwort plantain coarsely. Cut the aubergines, tomato and kohlrabi into cubes and slice the carrots thinly. Then chop the onion finely and fry in oil. Add carrots, aubergines and kohlrabi and season with the dried herbs. Then add the vegetable stock and the tomato purée and boil on medium heat for 15 minutes. Stir in the ribwort plantain and the tomato cubes and cook for a few more minutes. Finally add the cream, taste and season with salt. Serve with rice or potatoes.

Ribwort Plantain Savoury Cake

Serves 6 as a main course

This is not a sweet cake but a savoury main dish.

300 g whole-wheat flour
1 level tablespoon baking powder
3 eggs
1 cup whipping cream
150 g butter
2 tablespoons vegetable stock powder
1 teaspoon basil, dried
1 teaspoon marjoram, dried
1 teaspoon dill, dried
1 teaspoon chives, dried
salt, pepper
4 handfuls ribwort plantain

Mix the flour with the baking powder. Separate the eggs and whisk the egg whites until stiff. Whip the cream until stiff. Cream the egg yolks together with the soft butter.

Mix the vegetable stock powder, the dried herbs and the seasoning with the flour. Stir in the mixture of butter and eggs. Beat the mixture thoroughly.

Chop the ribwort plantain finely and add it to the mixture; then stir in the cream and fold the egg whites in.

Turn the mixture out into a greased cake tin and bake in the oven at 180°C (350°F, gas mark 4) for 40 minutes.

This cake looks quite wet and heavy before baking, but afterwards it is light and fluffy. It is best when served hot.

Ribwort Plantain-filled Peppers

Serves 4 as a main course

Vegetables
4 medium peppers (about 600 g)
4 large tomatoes (about 750 g)
1 large onion
olive oil for frying
250 g rice
375 ml vegetable stock
300 g ribwort plantain leaves
Sauce
1 onion
1-2 cloves garlic
1 tablespoon olive oil
2 tablespoons tomato purée
125 ml single cream
salt, pepper

For the vegetables, cut the peppers in a way that you can open a lid and remove the seeds. Open the tomatoes in the same way and remove the flesh and seeds with a spoon. Set them aside for the sauce. Cut the onion into very small cubes and fry it in a lot of oil until translucent. Add the rice and fry it, but keep stirring to prevent it from burning. Add the vegetable stock when the rice is translucent. Let simmer gently for 20 minutes. Five minutes before the rice is cooked add the finely chopped ribwort plantain to the rice.

For the sauce, cut another onion into small cubes and fry it together with the crushed garlic in oil until translucent. Stir in the tomato purée as well as the reserved flesh and seeds of the tomatoes. Cook for some time, stirring in the single cream little by little, thus thickening the sauce. Taste and season from time to time until the taste is right.

Spoon the rice mixture into the peppers, put the lids on top and arrange them in a greased ovenproof dish. Pour the sauce over the peppers and bake in the oven at 175°C (350°F, gas mark 4) for 35 minutes.

Young nipplewort

Silverweed
Potentilla anserina

96

Silverweed Gnocchi

Serves 4 as a main course

The silverweed should be very young with delicate stalks.

600 g potatoes
3 handfuls silverweed
1 small onion
butter for frying
1 egg
75 g flour
75 g semolina
pepper, nutmeg

 Boil and mash the potatoes. Chop the silverweed finely and fry it together with the chopped onion in butter. Purée the mixture.

Blend the weeds with the potatoes and add all the other ingredients. Knead them together and season with pepper and nutmeg. Flour a clean surface and form three rolls of the dough (each about 3 cm in diameter). Dust the rolls with flour and cut them into slices 5 mm thick. Each slice is formed into one gnocchi by placing it on a fork, gently pressing it with a finger and rolling it up a bit. Put the gnocchi on a floured tea towel.

Bring a large pot of salted water to the boil, put the gnocchi into the water, one portion at a time, and let simmer for 3 to 4 minutes. Take them out with the slotted spoon and leave to drain. Serve with a tomato sauce or a creamy white one.

Silverweed – very rich in vitamin C (see table on page 91).

Silverweed Butter Spread

The silverweed should be very young with delicate stalks.

200 g butter
1 handful silverweed
2 tablespoons yeast flakes
1 teaspoon vegetable stock powder
¹/₂ teaspoon coriander seed, finely ground
pepper

 The butter should be soft. Chop the silverweed very finely and blend it well into the butter. Then mix in the other ingredients. Serve on bread.

Weeds for kids

I am sure many mothers would like their children to eat highly nutritious weeds. This may be difficult, as children often do not want to eat things they do not know. So my tip is to chop them very finely like parsley, for example, and add them to salads or cream soups. You can use any weed like this.

Smooth Sow Thistle
Sonchus oleraceus

Smooth Sow Thistle Mushroom Filling

Serves 4 as a main course

A delicious vegetarian dish for a barbecue.

12 large mushrooms
lemon juice
75 g finely grated cheese
1 onion
2 cloves garlic
olive oil
150 g pearl barley
300 ml vegetable stock
2 good handfuls smooth sow thistle
1 tablespoon single cream
sesame seeds

Scrape out the mushrooms with a small teaspoon. Chop the contents and set aside. Squeeze lemon juice over the mushrooms and sprinkle some of the cheese inside. Chop the onion and the garlic finely and fry them in the oil until translucent. Add the barley and continue to fry. After 3 minutes add the vegetable stock. Chop the smooth sow thistle coarsely and stir it in, together with the reserved mushroom. Boil the mixture until most of the liquid has evaporated. Let the barley mixture cool slightly and purée with the blender. The paste should be thick. If it is too thin heat it in a pan, stirring all the time, until it thickens. Stir in the single cream. Mix the cheese into the hot purée. Spoon the paste into the mushrooms and sprinkle with sesame seeds. Wrap the mushrooms in tin foil, two to three at a time. Put the mushrooms on the grill or bake them in the oven at 200°C (400°F, gas mark 6) for 15 to 20 minutes.

Smooth Sow Thistle Spaghetti Sauce

Enough for 3 servings as a main course

Quick and easy!

 250 g smooth sow thistle leaves
3 onions
30 g butter
150 ml vermouth
200 g single cream
3 tablespoons grated Parmesan cheese
herb salt
500 g whole-wheat spaghetti

Wash the smooth sow thistle, remove the tough stalks and dry the leaves with a kitchen towel. Cut them in strips. Chop the onions very finely and fry them in butter until they are translucent. Add the weeds and the vermouth and cook for about 5 minutes. Keep stirring well, otherwise it might burn. Turn down to low heat and add the single cream. Simmer for 2 minutes. Finally add the cheese and season with herb salt. Boil the spaghetti until it is al dente and drain through a sieve. Mix with the vegetable sauce and serve immediately.

Smooth Sow Thistle Spread

200 g mushrooms
2 handfuls smooth sow thistle
4 tablespoons sunflower oil
salt, pepper
soy sauce
lemon juice

Chop mushrooms and sow thistle very finely and mix well together. Add the oil, salt and pepper, and blend it well into the mixture. Season with soy sauce and lemon juice. Serve on freshly baked bread.

Smooth Sow Thistle Dressing

2 handfuls smooth sow thistle
a few leaves ground ivy
a small bunch of chives
2 cloves garlic
juice of ½ lemon
1 tablespoon yeast flakes
2 tablespoons olive oil
a lettuce

Chop the weeds and the chives very finely and crush the garlic. Make a dressing of lemon juice, yeast flakes, garlic and oil. Mix the chopped herbs into the dressing and pour it over the prepared lettuce leaves. Blend well before serving.

Sorrel
Rumex acetosa

Sorrel Cream Soup

Sorrel contains a relatively high amount of oxalic acid. If it is consumed frequently it should be boiled up in water for a short time and drained before being processed. This will reduce the acid content.

1 large onion
butter for frying
1 heaped tablespoon whole wheat grains, finely ground into
  flour
500 ml water
2 good handfuls sorrel
1 heaped teaspoon vegetable stock powder
1 heaped teaspoon herb salt
pepper
100 g single cream

Chop the onion and fry it in butter until translucent. Remove from the heat and sprinkle in the flour. Reheat and add the water, stirring well. Add the sorrel and season with vegetable stock powder, pepper and salt. Let simmer for about 15 minutes. Remove the soup from the heat, let cool slightly and liquidize with the blender. Stir in the cream before serving.

Sorrel Millet Pudding

Serves 6

To reduce the acid content, see my previous note.

Pudding

4 medium onions
100 g millet
1 teaspoon curry powder
350 ml vegetable stock
200 g carrots
100 g Savoy cabbage
150 g sorrel
50 ml single cream
salt, nutmeg
3 eggs
200 g Gouda cheese

Sauce

50 g tomatoes
4 cloves garlic
a small bunch basil
butter for frying
1 heaped tablespoon tomato purée
100 ml red wine
1 tablespoon paprika
nutmeg
salt, pepper

Grease a pudding dish (one with a lid, 1500 ml capacity) and sprinkle the greased surface with semolina. Place it in the fridge. Chop the onions finely and fry them in butter until translucent. Stir in the millet and curry powder and add the vegetable stock. Cover and simmer on a low heat for 25 minutes, stirring from time to time.

In the meantime grate the carrots, chop the Savoy cabbage

very finely and the sorrel coarsely. Fry carrots and cabbage in butter, adding some water from time to time so that it does not burn. When they are nearly cooked stir in the sorrel and continue to cook for a short time. Add the single cream and season with salt and nutmeg. Remove the millet from the heat and leave to cool down a bit. Then gradually stir in 2 eggs and two-thirds of the cheese. Mix the third egg and the remaining cheese with the sorrel mixture.

Put two-thirds of the millet mixture into the pudding dish and make a well in the centre. Spoon the sorrel mixture into the well and cover with the remaining millet. Close the lid tightly, put into a steamer with enough boiling water. Boil for 1 ½ hours, making sure that no water gets into the pudding.

For the sauce, cut the tomatoes into cubes, crush the garlic and chop the basil finely. First fry the tomatoes in butter, then mix in garlic and basil. Add tomato purée, red wine and spices, then season and simmer for about 10 minutes.

Arrange slices of the millet pudding on plates, pour sauce over them and serve immediately.

Sorrel – one of our most common weeds.

Sorrel Spread

Delicious on sourdough bread and garnished with tomato slices. To reduce the acid content of sorrel, see my previous note.

300 g potatoes
2 tablespoons butter
3 tablespoons single cream
1 large onion
butter for frying
3 handfuls sorrel leaves
2 teaspoons tomato purée
herb salt and pepper
nutmeg

Boil the potatoes with skins on. When they are cooked purée them, adding butter and single cream. Chop the onion and fry it in some butter. When it is translucent add the sorrel. Fry on a low heat for about 5 minutes until it is a paste-like substance. Mix the creamed potatoes with the sorrel and stir in the tomato purée, herb salt, pepper and nutmeg.

Medicinal teas

Whether taking a weed or medicinal herb as a tea or in any other form it is important not to take them for longer than six weeks as many of them work very effectively as a medicine.

Spruce Syrup

This syrup can be used to spread on bread or when making a pudding or ice-cream.

 a few handfuls fresh spruce shoots
1 glass liquid honey

Fill a glass jar with a screw-on lid with the fresh spruce shoots. Pour honey over the shoots until they are fully covered. Screw the lid on tightly. Leave to stand for 6 weeks, then remove the shoots by straining through a sieve. The syrup can be stored for a couple of weeks.

Spruce Ice-Cream

 about 200 ml syrup made with spruce shoots (to one's own taste)
300 ml whipping cream

 Whip the cream until thick and sweeten with the syrup to taste. Freeze the cream.

Stinging Nettle
Urtica dioica

112

'Gourmet' Stinging Nettle Soup

Serves 4

When cooking stinging nettles it is important that you only use young leaves. The stalks are so tough and stringy that not even the blender can crush them. Wear gloves when picking and also when washing the stinging nettles in order to avoid getting stung.

500 g potatoes
2 onions
butter
1 litre hot vegetable stock
100 g stinging nettle leaves
2 teaspoons lemon juice
pepper, salt
200 ml whipping cream
50 g flaked almonds
1 large carrot

Wash the potatoes and cut them into cubes. Chop the onions and fry them in butter, together with the potatoes, until the onions are translucent. Add the hot vegetable stock, bring to boil and let everything simmer for 10 minutes. Wash the stinging nettles (using rubber gloves) and add the leaves to the soup. Cook for another 10 minutes. Let the soup cool slightly before liquidizing with the blender. Add the lemon juice and season with pepper and salt. Stir in 100 ml cream. Whip the remaining cream and put it aside. Roast the flaked almonds in a pan without fat until they are light brown. Grate the carrot finely.

Serve in soup plates, finished with some whipped cream and the almonds and grated carrot sprinkled on top.

Stinging Nettle Pie

Serves 4 as a main course

See the note about cooking stinging nettles in the previous recipe.

250 g wholemeal wheat flour
250 g butter
250 g quark
1-2 cloves garlic
1 large onion
oil for frying
1 teaspoon ground nutmeg
$^1/_2$ teaspoon chilli powder
pepper
1 kg stinging nettle tips
2-3 tablespoons vegetable stock powder
500 g tomato passata
a small amount of finely ground whole-wheat flour

Knead flour, butter and quark together to make a smooth dough. Allow to rest in the fridge for at least half an hour. Finely chop the garlic and the onion. Fry in oil until golden brown. Add the spices and the pepper but take care not to burn. Wash the stinging nettles and chop them coarsely. Mix them with the onions and add the vegetable stock powder. After 5 minutes stir in the tomato passata and let simmer until cooked. If the paste is too dry add some water; if it is too thin, sprinkle some flour over it and stir it in. Roll out one-third of the dough and cover the bottom of a greased spring-form tin with it. Use the second third to form a rim. Spoon in the vegetable mixture. Cover it with a lid of the remaining dough and prick it with a fork. Bake in the oven at 200°C (400°F, gas mark 6) for 30 minutes.

Stinging Nettle Rissoles

Serves 4 as a main course

See my note about cooking stinging nettles in the first nettle recipe.

1 onion
oil for frying
150 g stinging nettles
100 g coarsely ground green spelt
50 g finely ground green spelt
500 ml vegetable stock
2 eggs
3 tablespoons Parmesan cheese
pepper

Chop the onion finely and fry in the oil until translucent. Chop the stinging nettle leaves finely, add them to the onion and cook for 5 minutes. Stir the green spelt into the saucepan, add the vegetable stock and bring to the boil. Boil the mixture for 15 minutes, stirring from time to time. Add water if it becomes too thick and to avoid burning. Leave to cool a bit, then add eggs, cheese and pepper. Shape small rissoles and fry them in hot oil.

Stinging nettle

Only use young leaves because the stalk is very tough. Wear gloves whilst picking and washing the nettles. The seeds of the nettle can be pulled off carefully and eaten raw – they are delicious. They can also be added to salads. The seeds can be dried for the winter to be sprinkled over salads.

NB only eat the seeds (not the leaves) raw otherwise you will sting your mouth. This is very unpleasant but not

Stinging Nettle Mushroom Paste

You can use this paste as a spread, a dip or even as basis for a salad dressing. But see the notes about cooking stinging nettles.

 3 medium potatoes
2–3 handfuls stinging nettle leaves
1 small handful ground ivy
2 onions
200 g mushrooms
butter for frying
1 tablespoon single cream
2 tablespoons yeast flakes
pepper, salt
$^1/_2$ teaspoon paprika

Scrub and steam the potatoes. Chop the stinging nettle leaves coarsely and the ground ivy finely. Boil them in water for 5 minutes, and then pour the water away. Chop the onions and the mushrooms and fry them in butter. Cream the potatoes (with skin on, if you like), the weeds and the mushrooms together in the blender. Stir in the cream and the yeast flakes. Taste and season with pepper, salt and paprika. Store the paste in the fridge, it will keep for a couple of days.

116

Stinging Nettle Spread

See my notes about using stinging nettles before undertaking this recipe.

1 large onion
250 g butter
4 good handfuls stinging nettle leaves
2 cloves garlic
1 teaspoon vegetable stock powder
2 tablespoon tomato purée
nutmeg
pepper

Chop the onion finely and fry in a small amount of the butter until translucent. Chop the stinging nettle leaves very finely, crush the garlic and add both to the onions. Add the vegetable stock powder, the tomato purée, nutmeg and pepper to the weeds and cook for 15 minutes. Cool slightly, then liquidize with the blender. Return to pan. Finally add the rest of the butter and warm up until it is soft and you can stir it in. Serve on freshly baked bread.

Stinging nettle – only pick the tops off.

Wild Garlic
Allium ursinum

118

Wild Garlic Tsatsiki

Serves 4 as a first course

Wild garlic is related to garlic, it can be found between March and May in woods and hedgerows. It has a much more intense taste if you use the green leaves as well as the white stalks.

30 g wild garlic
a small bunch of chives
1 ¹/₂ onions
¹/₂ cucumber
250 g full-fat quark
200 g yoghurt
herb salt
pepper
1 clove garlic (optional)

Chop the wild garlic and the chives finely. Cut the onions into small cubes and grate the cucumber coarsely. Mix the quark well with half of the yoghurt and add the prepared ingredients. Mix in the second half of the yoghurt and stir until the mixture is smooth. Taste and season with pepper and salt. Add some crushed garlic if you prefer your tsatsiki to be more pungent.

Wild Garlic Soup with Croûtons

Serves 2

150 g wild garlic
1 large onion
butter
2 sage leaves
¹/₂ teaspoon ground cloves
250 ml vegetable stock
1 tablespoon flour
250 ml single cream
pepper and herb salt
2 thin slices of whole-wheat bread
fat for frying

Chop the wild garlic very finely and cut the onion into very small cubes. Fry wild garlic and onion in butter until the onion cubes are translucent. Then add sage leaves and ground cloves. Add the vegetable stock and bring to the boil. Let the mixture simmer for a few minutes. Let the soup cool slightly, then liquidize with the blender. Put the flour into a shaker, add a small amount of cold water and shake well. Stir this mixture into the soup and bring to the boil again, stirring all the time until the soup is creamy. Now add the single cream and taste. Season with pepper and herb salt.

Cut the bread slices into croûtons. Heat some fat in a frying pan and fry until crisp. Sprinkle the croûtons over the soup.

Wild Garlic Vol-au-vents

Serves 4 as a main course, or 8 as a first course

250 g wild garlic
50 g butter
some water
4 tablespoons flour
250 ml single cream
250 ml milk
3 teaspoons vegetable stock powder
pepper
$^1/_2$ teaspoon chilli powder
8 vol-au-vent cases

Chop the wild garlic very finely. Fry it in butter until tender, adding some water from time to time so that it does not burn. Sprinkle on the flour and blend it well into the wild garlic. Slowly add cream and milk, stirring all the time. Season with vegetable stock powder, pepper and chilli powder. Set the oven to 200°C (400°F, gas mark 6) and warm the vol-au-vent cases for about 10 minutes. If the filling is too thick stir in some milk or water before you spoon it into the vol-au-vent cases. Serve immediately.

Wild Garlic Butter Spread

You can deep-freeze wild garlic but it will lose some of its strong taste. At the same time other frozen food will take on its aroma, therefore make sure it is stored in an airtight container. The leaves should be chopped before deep-freezing or when still frozen, because afterwards it is difficult to cut them.

200 g butter
200 g wild garlic
pepper
herb salt
nutmeg

The butter should be soft and smooth. Chop the wild garlic very finely. Mix the leaves into the soft butter. Taste and add seasoning and the nutmeg. Serve on bread or toast.

Wild garlic – the flower has the strongest taste.

Yarrow
Achillea millefolium

Yarrow Polenta with Almond Crust

Serves 4 as a main course

800 ml vegetable stock
200 g polenta
2 large onions
4 handfuls yarrow
2 cloves garlic
butter
pepper
nutmeg
200 g flaked almonds
butter

Bring the vegetable stock to the boil and add the polenta. Let simmer on a low heat for 10 to 15 minutes, stirring all the time. Chop the onions and the yarrow finely and crush the garlic. Fry it all together in butter and season with pepper and nutmeg. Sauté the almonds in some butter until golden, but take care not to burn them. Fill a greased ovenproof dish with alternate layers of polenta and vegetables. Sprinkle the almonds on top. Bake in the oven at 200°C (400°F, gas mark 6) for 20 to 25 minutes.

Yarrow Masala

Serves 2 as a main course

The cooking time of yarrow depends on the age of the plant: young, delicate parts are cooked quickly. Do not use the tough stalks of older plants but only the leaves.

300 g carrots
300 g kohlrabi
2 onions
oil for frying
2 cloves garlic
2 tablespoons desiccated coconut
2 teaspoons ground coriander seed
2 teaspoons cumin powder
1 teaspoon ground ginger
1 teaspoon turmeric
$^1/_2$ teaspoon chilli powder
250 ml salted water
4 handfuls yarrow
200 g yoghurt
4 tablespoons single cream

Cut the carrots and kohlrabi into small cubes. Chop the onions finely and fry them in oil. Crush the garlic and add it together with the coconut and all the spices. Fry for a short time, stirring well. Mix in carrots and kohlrabi and add the water. Cook for about 20 minutes. After 10 minutes add the finely chopped yarrow and continue to cook. Finally add yoghurt and cream and bring to the boil again. Remove from the heat and serve with rice.

Yarrow and Mixed Vegetables

Serves 4 as a main course

150 g green spelt
400 ml vegetable stock
300 g aubergines
2 medium onions
200 g courgettes
200 g carrots
2 tomatoes
6 handfuls young yarrow or yarrow leaves
100 g Savoy cabbage
2 large cloves garlic
2-3 tablespoons olive oil
salt, pepper

Simmer the green spelt in the vegetable stock for 20 minutes. Drain off the liquid and set aside. In the meantime cut the aubergines into cubes. Chop the onions finely, cut the courgettes and carrots into cubes, and slice the tomatoes. Chop up the yarrow finely and cut the cabbage into thin strips. Crush the garlic. Fry the onions and aubergines in oil, stirring well. Add cabbage and carrots. Keep stirring and mix in garlic and courgettes. If the mixture is too dry, add some of the liquid from the green spelt. Finally add the yarrow and the tomatoes. Season and cook until all the ingredients are tender (about 20 minutes in all). Serve the vegetables mixed with the green spelt.

Yarrow Pancake Dream

Serves 4 as a main course

2 eggs
250 ml milk
100 g flour
salt
oil for frying
1 large onion
3 handfuls yarrow
2 cloves garlic
500 g tomatoes
butter for frying
4 tablespoons tomato purée
1 teaspoon basil
1 tablespoon vegetable stock powder
1 pinch chilli powder
700 g grated Gouda cheese

Make a batter of eggs, milk, flour and salt, let it rest, then make 6 pancakes, fried in oil for about 2 minutes on each side. Chop the onion and the yarrow finely, crush the garlic and cut the tomatoes into cubes. Fry the onion in butter for 2 to 3 minutes, then add garlic and tomatoes and continue to fry for a short time. Stir in the yarrow. Add tomato purée, basil, vegetable stock and chilli powder. Simmer for about 10 minutes. Grease a baking tray and place a pancake in the centre. Spread the vegetable sauce on it and sprinkle some cheese on. Put the next pancake on top and repeat the procedure with all remaining pancakes. The top layer of the 'tower' should be grated cheese. Bake in the oven at 200°C (400°F, gas mark 6) for about 20 minutes.

Yarrow – do not use the stalk, only the leaves that are soft.